The Valley of the Tutuilla, and Other Lines

A Collection of Published Poems

Dorys Crow Grover

The Valley of the Tutuilla, and Other Lines

Library of Congress
Catalog Card No. 97-94298

ISBN 1-57579-085-8

Printed in United States of America

PINE HILL PRESS, INC.
Freeman, S. Dak. 57029

Table of Contents

The Valley of the Tutuilla

When we lived in the valley,
below the spacing hills,
where the larks sang at sunset,
and our hearts sang too,
it was a time for listening
in the clear blue air,
for the Angelus of evening.
O, we listened there.

Trees were so few, so rare,
in the Tutuilla valley,
we felt anxious about them:
a willow bending solitary
along the dry stream;
cottonwood groves blending,
swaying like summer dresses do,
when girls go dancing.

When we lived in the valley,
the rising blue mountains,
spread forever eastward,
surrounding the little Mission,
a refuge through the years,
when the Cayuse rode their ponies,
through the rye grass and sage,
O, they heard the Angelus.

When we lived in the valley,
our world was a quiet place.
The seasons made yearly trips;
bringing mysteries to us there,
and in the shifting currents,
our brief lives seemed a whim,
of time and space and sun.
O, we heard the Angelus then.

Meadowlark Over Tutuilla

Just at dusk the Meadowlark wings
in along the Tutuilla.
The bird's rise is yellow-breasted.
It wears a black gorget,
and sings into the silence
like choral bells at night.
Listen for the trilling,
splitting air-wave sound;
the dance, the glory, the majesty
of its being and its flight.
Flushed from the water's edge,
it rises above this field,
and dips momentarily before
flashing off into the wild.

Waiilatpu

You can still hear the guns
in far Umatilla's canyons,
land of the Walla Wallas,
the Nez Perce and Cayuse.
Silent in the long
stretch of time, they lie
together in the Waiilatpu,
where the river runs west.

You can still hear the war cries,
rising above the battle dust,
where Whirlwind and Yellow Hawk
rode away with the Great Spirit
leaving behind the burning
memory of fearless warriors,
where the river runs west,
through the Waiilatpu.

[In Cayuse Waiilatpu means "place of the rye grass," or "where the rye grass grows."]

The Washita

for Helen Winter Stauffer

The poetry of the wind
came swirling down
across the Panhandle
like Custer's troops,
marching through the night
to massacre the Cheyenne
camped peacefully on the Washita
that time, when the white flag
of surrender fluttered,
and Old Glory signaled peace,
where Black Kettle died.

I have seen the dust of stars
in the eyes of the dead,
who believed in the promises,
and where the pathways led.
Although ages now have passed:
many snows in the burn of time,
nothing has dimmed the stars
nor slowed the ticking mind,
nor lifted the bones long
lingering on the wind's song,
where Black Kettle died.

Thames Fishermen

On the banks of the Thames,
you have seen the old men
sitting with shining eyes
and long thin poles, fishing,
sometimes till dark,
sometimes into the night.
They sit in silence in the shadows.
I wonder if the fish ever bite,
swimming there below,
near the paved banks.

I have seen them sitting
downriver from the bridge,
where loaded grain barges
pass at all hours, day and night,
breaking light from the waves,
churning up the river's peace.

I prefer to watch the old men,
their heads bent against the wind
that sweeps from the towers in the east,
bringing the cold, swift rain,
shining the ancient stones.
The men hold their supple reeds
while slow time moves, and
their strong dark faces
hide secrets from the light.

Père Lachaise

This bare Parisian winter day,
the old tombs on the wooded hill
seem heaped together,
encircled in the whisper
of the trees' long boughs.
Under gray marble, in repose,
the giants rest in chamber rows.
Here lies Chopin, Colette and Moliere,
and there in vaults, half over-grown
with ivy, rest Abelard and Heloise.
Balzac scans the fair city,
and there is Wilde's Egyptian crypt:
Remark the mutilation!
Among the marble slabs upright
the solitary wild cats linger,
their eyes curious and fine,
surveying their vast domain,
as Satan might, under the eye of God,
ponder each giant's fate.
Here the workers of human comedy rest.
Seasons go. Seasons come.
Poppies bend red nodders
in the summer's sun,
but on this cold winter day,
these guests all in ruin lie.

Gallarus Oratory

This shelter of ancient prayer
is set in a field of stone,
and looks like a beehive,
with its strange corbel- roof
sloping toward the earth;
as if kneeling of itself,
on Ireland's sacred ground.

The winds and rains
of thousands of years,
have battered this stronghold;
a little cross-pillared hermitage,
it was a refuge of solitude.

I stand before the open door,
through which the ages have passed,
and wonder about those souls
who tarried here alone
in that long- remembered time.

Strasbourg

They call her *la belle Européenne!*
She lies restless and lovely
across the spreading Rhine:
Strasbourg *l'élégante!*
Here the great cathedral rises,
a symbol of her charm.

Have you seen the cloisters
in the afternoon, before tea?
The sun slants through the arcades,
and all along the high walls
bees sing in the vines
where dust motes dance
until the shadows of evening
fall across the stones
where horsemen ride on high.

Then bells in the towers
mark the hours when time,
like a thief, hastes away,
and lovers begin the race
before their passions die,
in *la belle Européenne.*

A Baltic Storm

Sometimes the music goes deep
    inside and hurts the beauty
    it brings.
When I hear the song, I am again
    walking along a street
    in a Bavarian town.

The light is going and dusk
    is coming with the rain,
    sweeping down from the Alps.

Wien, wien, nur du allein . . .

How haunting is the melody that
    comes from the Rathaus,
    glorious in age.
Miles away, I remember how the rain
    fell at Timmendorfer Strand,
    and from the tea room
in the SeeSchlosschen, we watched
    the storm; the women sewing
    in the Strandkorbs, laughing.
Before the wind brought the rain
    from the sea and the Baltic
    splashed cold over the sand;
how it raged, and the tea was hot,
    and we were happy in the great
    Baltic hotel by the sea.

Wien, wien, nur du allein . . .

Miles and miles away in memory
    across another ocean,
    the melody lingers on.
There is another sweet voice singing:
    the song of a meadow lark
    in a wheat field in the West.
And the light is going and dusk
    is coming with the rain
    sweeping down from the mountains.

The Fountain in Nantes

Bacchic revellers and elegant ladies,
some reclining, some upright
and stern, and all dripping wet,
grace the ancient fountain
of Place Royale in Nantes,
near the great Cathedral,
where Jesus stands with an utterly
blank expression, holding the keys
to the Kingdom of Heaven—
the promise of true justice.

Here in this ancient city
on an old theatre wall—
do not miss the three figures
standing *troupe l'oeill* on a balcony:
a muse, a young woman, and a lad,
so small he stands on books
to view the dancers across the way.
Une tres joyeux group!

The Choral Society

Last summer one night
moored by *la Belle Anquille*,
at a waterside inn near Redon
[in Brittany],
I thought about Bogie
romancing Bergman
in the Paris-Hollywood Inn
called Casablanca.

Then in the dim light,
sixteen local school teachers
on holiday suddenly
burst into glorious song.

And later, just as suddenly
when I was looking through
a port hole of the boat
the sun, a fuzzy, uncertain
half-asleep blur of gold,
spread across what looked to me
like Van Gogh's hayfields.
Through the abeles
lining the canal towpath,
a white mist lay on the water,
and for a few minutes
the world was perfect.

Sometimes life is like that.
Especially in the Old World.
We know so little of these places
where some of us began once. Like
where the water wheel turns slowly
in the river near the ancient bridge
at the romantic *Moulin de l'Abbaye*
in Brantome.

I remember one time
when a beautiful woman
in full-length evening dress
swam in the sea. She said"
"The salt water will set the dye!"

And other places to recall;
where the Counts of Arlatan
lived specious lives in
a fifteenth-century mansion,
now a hotel in Arles. And
the Grenadines: here to stay—
small islands at the world's end;
the rainbow before the summer's fall—
my heart's pot-of-gold.

Mrs. Verey's Garden

I saw aging spring pass
in the misty noon,
listening to the silence
that is the garden's.
I was stunned by colors
of natural wonder:
drooping Laburnam's yellow glow,
and the soft, light shade
along so many pathways,
my heart was lifted
like hounds to afternoon.
I wandered and drifted,
like a person aswoon,
among the glories there,
locking them all inside,
where secrets are apt to hide.
The stranger as I passed
cast a wary eye.
The road of life is wide,
though dying, it will last.

These Owls

There were these owls—see.
They would be resting
on the main beam
in the big red barn,
where the fork pulley moves
the bales of hay along.
When we climbed up to the loft,
they would fly across
the great open haymow,
and wing away through
the broken windows,
out into the fields and sage,
into the night's caress
trapped in the passageways
of unlimited darkness.

Often I have come into the barn,
after a summer rain
came suddenly from the west,
and found them there
sitting in quiet repose.

Sometimes in the blue center of night,
after the moon stumbles into the sky
you can see them there,
over your left shoulder,
white against the rafters,
quiet, moving slightly
toward your blue center,
watching, heads turning,
with curious wide eyes.

Standing there in mild surmise,
I wonder if they're really wise!

The Ranch on the Limpia

As I was passing by the ruins
of an old ranch house,
I chanced upon a letter, torn
but legible, and dated 1889.
It read, in part, "He said today
We had been here Twenny years,
And I began to cry, Dear Mother,
Because I do not believe that we
Are like to see Each Other any more . . ."

I tell this story years hence.
of how he built the ranch house
in a canyon along Limpia Creek
in the Trans-Pecos,
where the dark green cedars grow on
clay-loam hills and rugged bluffs.
The stage road passes nearby,
fleeing daily toward Fort Davis
from the rolling staked plains.

Mountains rise with every dawn,
but she never sees the sky,
nor the water-rushing creek,
nor the wind-tossed trees,
for she waits day and night—
watches even while she works—
waits to have the first sight
of a traveler passing by.

The hypocritic days linger,
and the long nights
fill her world with silence,
or the wild coyote's song.
She leans on the window sill,
passing the hours.
One day, when pounding hoofs rang
against her swirling thoughts,

she never gave a sign.
The winters were always the worst.
Snow keeps everything distant,
and he found her drifting
farther and farther away.

[This poem won the Centennial Writing Competition Award given by Fort Concho Museum Press, San Angelo, TX, during its second annual Literary Festival, August 1989. It was printed in the ***Fort Concho Report,*** winter edition].

Waitsburg Cemetery

These cemetery gates are open.
I stand beside the plot
of her life: 1866-1939.
This is my progenitor:
Anglo-Welsh-Dutch.
She had three husbands;
one related to me.
My father's mother, she
lived in her own happiness,
bearing seven: he was the last,
and they have all passed
through the open gate.

Here in this country of buried souls,
there must be a lot of stories
that run backward to fading,
with time for failures
forgotten or condoned.
She is dismissed with a name and a date,
carved in a faltering of stone.

The Rainbow Trail

Praise be for the silver flashes
on the brown speckled gray
of the plashing flourish
in midstream rush,
wrought suddenly of change
by the rainbow's astonishment.

> This railing I lean on
> has years of history.
> Guarded in old stone,
> I cannot tell its secrets,
> so recent am I
> in the nature of things.

A line of blue shoots away
across the surging stream
of my colorful reverie,
for the lure, like promised love,
is taken on faith and flips
the river bed into turmoil.

> The reeds dancing along the shore
> in seasonal gaiety,
> sway unlaced messages
> to rainbows everywhere,
> here under the old stone bridge.

Praise be for the sweeping curve,
the bending grass, the furl
that lengthens in the shadows
along the rainbow trail:
resting, gathered, waiting,
below the silent stones.

Loony

Wrapped in goose down,
under the stately pines,
I never begrudge them
the sleep they cost me.
I lie awake listening
to their wild, discordant calls,
which begin at a distance
in a spruce-bound lake cove,
and travel the starry air
like the pressure booms
of January ice on a pond.
Echoes build. Then other
birds join their chorus.
Such mad music,
pounded in minor keys
by these moonstruck organists!
It is no wonder they are called
the wild, crazy loons.

The Lone Heron

Let me tell you how the mist
rises—
above the pond at dawn,
and how a lone white heron
came winging,
full feathers folded.
How it sailed in on the wind
coming up from the raging gulf,
ahead of the hurricane's
heedless crush;
how it splash-landed
scattering crystals
of fine shattered glass;
how it coasted into the misty day.
Lost? Perhaps having not paused here
before—
it gleams brightly on the pond.

Let me tell you how the sun comes
side-slipping through the oaks;
how the garrulous mockingbirds
have spread the morning news
through the shifting gauzy air.
Having voyaged from the tempest,
the bird on long thin legs,
wades through the reeds,
watching the ducks loafing . . . serene.

An Angle of Geese

A high, haunting, almost imperceptible call
has them listening, straining upward,
searching, cupping hands to ears.
There they are! The first geese of autumn,
wedging their way through the outer
fringes of our trivial day,
connecting us to the higher reaches
of dreams; the promise of constancy:
the proof of faith, flying South.

Old men and little children,
where old men and little children
are fortunate enough to live in silent places,
run into their yards in the evening
to watch the first geese fly
against the autumn moon in rippling V's.
Angled into the thin edge of night,
their cries telling a story of the wild
in the sky's blue-broken brow.

The old men and little children
stand and stare at the star-crossed sky,
moon-wrapped in the silver evening
holding against their hearts
the close mystery of truth,
cutting through the vast space
scattering the dust of heaven,
while we sleep dreaming of horses,
pacing the Elysian Fields.

The Wild Ducks of Maloy

The trees starting their annual rush,
primp themselves in raiment lush.
The paths are wet, the pools fresh,
and under April's stormy eye,
mirrors reflect all nature's array;
and one small brook impatiently,
swirls about the ducks of Maloy.

My seventieth spring has come,
since first I started count,
and before I am well finished—done,
lovers will pass a younger fount.
Oh! Our hearts are growing old,
we meet each season with such pain,
even ducks may weep in the rain.

But now I drift and laze away,
beneath the sun's bright stare,
I know I'm moving every day,
though I meet them with a dare,
it seems that time did dissipate
all of my heart's desires,
and left me only ducks too late.

Riders of the Storm

Petrels are small sea birds.
Melville knew of them.
Wing-dipped in flight,
they seem to gather and spread,
like seeds a farmer casts
when he sows a meadow.
Grouped and surging on the wind,
they swim the steady space
of a world when June chills
their Antarctic breeding place.

Named for the Apostle,
they walk the waves on webbed feet,
portending storms.
Sailors bewail their arrival,
believing they hold the souls
of drowned companions.
The truth is—
attracted by the ship's lights,
they drop onto the decks at night,
utter ghostly cackles,
and sponge a free ride!

Spiders

Here in the narrow dark,
the spiders are weaving
their thin threads,
sewing up the day
in their private suites,
webbed in myriad trails.
Their strong borders
catch my heart's fancy.
In the dark crevasses
where light dimly lies,
they reach out with care.
I reach in carefully.
We know each other,
the spiders and I.

Lis d'un jour

Where I live the day lily
is unfailingly a July flower.
Orange blossoms furl like flags
flying on Independence Day.
Old fashioned, there is scarcely
an old house without its blooms
under a window sill.
Farm wives long ago
must have found them a favorite.
They had little time for cultivating,
what they could not eat. And,
the French of Canada say of them:
Lis d'un jour.
For their time is a single day.
Sending forth bright fires:
a scrap of summer color
in brevity.

Mother's Place

I don't know that you've ever been there.
Far up the mountain is Mother's Place.
This morning on our way,
dawn was just lighting the eastern hills.
I watched a fainting sun push through
the dark to highlight the white-capped
Seven Devil Mountains.
Hemingway also knew these—
probably watched as amber color turns
the frozen land to gold.
Great rags of cloud torn by a rising wind,
brought spun snow like cotton candy
that sticks and stays,
blinding the pines, deep canyons, and us.

Mother lives on Cold Spring Ridge.
It's a steep route any time,
but with snow and ice along the bluff,
we sometimes wish she'd move to town
where it seems a little less dangerous.
But then I guess she's safer
on the Ridge with bears and mountain
lions than some other places we know.
In the woods where the great cedars
kneel as if praying for spring,
a lone owl swoops low
to see if we are easy prey.
It's a long way up the mountain
to Mother's Place.

A Prairie Town

In a willow flat
back of the grain elevators,
the lights of town gleam weakly,
like crumbled foxfire.
I ride along a dark lane
that rises to the prairie.
The eastern sky lies folded
like the cover on a bed,
and the stubble fields gleam
like harvested gold
under the summer moon.
It is a land of skylines
rising beyond the mind
and blending into the
mysterious silent giants;
the lonely elevators,
reaching into the air,
hovering over the fields,
the lane, and the town
which lies winking
in a willow flat.
And I, on the horse, riding alone,
wistful under the night's eye,
lonely as the elevators.

Prairie Creek

A touch of frost
feathers the brown grass
along the bottoms.
The sky runs west.
The short winter days are here.
Snow will soon cover the fields
when the new storm arrives,
flawing out like the tails
of white horses running.
The wind will pant and blow
against the windows.
Prairie Creek will be cut off
from the world. Alone.
A ragged flight of geese
angles south, crying;
a wavering V barely visible.
Theirs is a melancholy sound
because they signal winter.
In the high country and canyons,
the dark blue mountains
brace themselves before
slowly bending white.

My Old Eden

There is something about a horse
that brings Eden in;
rekindles an old, wild, stubborn
natural companionship.
Machines disconnect and
horses connect what is left,
of a kind of "free servitude,"
with pride and a toss of mane,
beginnings built on natural order.
The shy, archaic manner
of promise and hope and wonder
that comes of willing surrender,
and bends the trace
to the necessity of encounter.
There is something about a horse
that brings Eden in.

The Crossbow

Down by the river
I often hear a voice calling.
My late progenitor used
to make a joke of it.
She used to say, “Our ancient ones
descended from the branch,
became experts with the crossbow
and had the souls of artists.”
But what has that to do
with the voice of the river?
It is mysterious.
Like morning darkness, or
evening sunshine or—
or a moon never setting, or
even two moons—blue moons.
Whoever the singer,
calling from the stream,
it is often with trembling
I listen and dream
of that wondrous past.

The Wallowas

The Nez Perce once camped here
among the cottonwoods,
leafless now along the creek.
I stare out the narrow window
of this "assisted living" facility
called Alpine House,
into the wide spaces, recalling
Chief Joseph and his love
for these mountains
where Prairie Creek
swirls with fallen leaves.
Cornstalks rustle
in a deserted field
where his ponies once grazed.

They didn't let him stay
here below Ruby Peak,
which I can't see
from my resting place,
but they named a mountain
for him, and cut the Douglas
Firs and Ponderosa Pines.

The snows still come
as always, before and after
the Nez Perce were driven out.
And there are still memories.
Autumn is very special
in the Wallowa canyons.
From atop Chief Joseph mountain,
you can see the shining
Seven Devils Range
skirting the Idaho skyline.

No wonder he died of a broken heart,
so far from his majestic land.
My heart aches too. Especially

when I know I will never again
ride the high country.
But a campfire still burns
in my heart, and beyond the curtains
I can still see Eagle Cap
blushing rose-white at dawn. And
often I hear the horse bells
from the lower valley.

A Drama of the Gods

for John Graves

I watched the patient sky.
From the southwest they came.
Rolling to meet the blue-dark cloud's
charge: enormous shapes moving.
Dusk lingered on the horizon.
and through the trees yet bare,
I saw them meet with thunder,
and flash aloft spectacularly,
as the last red tints of sundown
flame-edged their fight.

There was nothing rational about it.
Furiously they spewed and roared.
Big drops of rain slashed diagonally
across the windswept land,
and lightning streaked white
in violent spears of light
that could have spawned theology.
It was a drama of the gods
and they put on quite a show,
as shows the gods put on go!

The Marshes

A smart breeze came leaping
over the flooding marshes.
Running through the sea grasses;
a steady, siffling, sighing rustle.
O subtle wind music!
Rather like the hum of gnats,
with rhythmic little flick aside.
A kind of peaceful euphoria
creeps into the mind,
soporific and indifferent
to all else in the world,
and the listener is enchanted
with a light-sight-haunted land,
where the sea crawls snakelike
across the moving sand
and sea grasses in the wind.

Old River

Your winding, meandering length,
stretching across continents,
is like a lecture in history,
though where you go
the thrush sings
and the tall pines dwell.
You run in dangerous waves,
lifting your singing voice
[often though you growl],
like a choir in a cathedral,
tuned to the currents rush
the willow's side-slipping
leafy soft whisper.

Through the drifting centuries,
when Redmen churned your blood,
when the trapper barged
and explorers split your dancing face,
searching for a hundred dreams,
you passed the everlasting days,
wandering with the wandering,
always constant and westward fleeing,
you admitted other streams; filled bays.

A life-giving journey you make
until even your strength is fragile,
as gasping you drown in the sea.

Cañon Adobe

The cañons turn between cliffs
a weary hand must have formed.
    Adobe,
    red and brown.
They rise and fall and lean
    gathering depth.

The great bald eagle finds
the Olympian heights.
    Poised,
    eyes shelved,
it takes piercing
    sheer-down falls.

Doves burst in a flutter
of gray feathers.
    Heavenward,
    on white wings.
Comrades in frightened
    splendor.

Paso Por Aqui

Passed here, travelers . . .

    Castenada

        Cabeza de Vaca

Onate

    Others.

The five levels of the pueblo
stand where the wind sings,
carving signs in the adobe,
marking lines in stone,

    where the piñons bend
    from the westward wind;

    where the women sing
    in the corn rows;

    where a child cries
    in the evening;

    where the sun sets
    in the azure . . .

Here people live; here people die.
Paso por aqui.

Little Rainland

This is desert land.
Rolling in sand and moving,
smoothing, when the wind blows,
like a woman trying
at her dressing table
to erase time
past.

This desert is old,
face sun-seared,
turning the grass brown-under,
drying the thin air hot
with stabbing sun-darts,
and setting a flood of color,
with a magnificent sweep of brush,
like a painter at an easel,
sketching shadows full.

This is face-weathered land,
cracked and broken tracts,
some misguided mystic made,
and then flung aside like
a faded worn mistress
with burning eyes.

Stovepipe Wells

It's the discovery of a place
that gives it a name.
Take for instance, Stovepipe Wells.
It's a little western town.
You can get there from Death Valley,
for it lies below the Panamint Mountains
which have white tops most winters.

As for its name: Stovepipe Wells.
Seems some forty-miner,
or prospector earlier or later,
didn't find gold, but water
[more important in a desert],
and the old or young explorer
marked the spot with a stovepipe.
All he had, I guess.

If you think the world
is becoming too populated,
take a trip to Stovepipe Wells,
across the desert from Tonopah.
Get high on scenery—
space will grow on you!

The Cheyenne

Trails from the four winds
cross at Lame Deer Creek,
final home of Black Wolf,
He Dog and Two Moons.
Here on the snow-cold slope,
beyond the white man's Fort,
many great warriors lie:
Little Wolf and Morning Star.

It was here Two Moons
surrendered in 1877.
White Bull betrayed them;
scalpled his old friend
Lame Deer. And the boy.
The shadows of unsung heroes
lengthen under the pines
on the hills above Lame Deer.

To My Author

from Monahseetah

A vehoe with pale eyes,
you have told my story,
while I walk along a river.
In choosing to do this
you have taken me,
and my People,
and placed us eternally
between white pages.

I stand on the river bank
listening to the voices
of my fathers, Little Rock,
Black Kettle and White Antelope,
and what I hear, listening,
you have inscribed forever,
our lives and deaths
between white pages.

You have visited my lodge;
still, you are a stranger to me.
I forgive you your trespass,
but I choose to walk
alone, along the river
in the place of my belonging,
while you spread my story
between white pages.

Someday when you return
to my story, I will walk
beside your flowing pen,
dipped in the living river
of my life you have captured,
like flashes of gleaming silver,
and fashioned in words
between white pages.

A Note from Monahseetah

You are still writing about me
bringing my people back,
making a whole rainbow
of life never before
put into the color of words.
My people went to the river
of bitter memory.
I have missed them.
Now your bird-like tracks
run across the white pages
to keep my story alive.
The years of my snows
are gray with eyes like
the fallen on the Washita
when the snow was red.

Keep writing down the mystery
of the years of my snows.

Ácoma

Long long ago,
from these amazing balconies,
hung in this incredible sky,
the people must have seen
the Spanish explorers pass
through the valley hundreds
of feet below, and laughed:
    their women safe,
    and their gold secure.

The landscape is a shimmering
reality with far away mountains.
This far south, a thousand years
have not changed much.
Upon the great plaza,
built somehow by careful hands,
the midday sun caresses
the brown adobe homes.
Here the lovely people
in scattered peace, cross
open plains where yet today
the land runs with yellow chamisa,
to green mountain pines.
With the sun this high,
a lone piñon strikes a pose.
Within its shadow I sit,
drawing lines in the sand,
dreaming of that early time,
of dust and sky and sun.

    A steep path,
    remnant of that ancient time,
    leads toward and away
    from the place where death once
    stilled the rush of blood.

The small winds chase
gray clouds across the courtyard
where ruins under the turquoise sky,
lie peaceful in space,
and enormous steps
climb upward in thin mountain air.

Sudden Shelter

There in the central Utah plateau
where a canyon drains eastward to Colorado,
prehistoric populations once thrived
millions of years ago.

What is the mystery of their disappearance?
Was it exploding supernovae?
Cosmic radiation?
Changing temperatures?
Extra-terrestrial wipe-out?
Drifting continents or rising mountains?

THE DINOSAUR

In her time she was beautiful.
Rising from the waters
with mud and slime
pouring from her two-story hips,
her great heavy body,
shining in the sunlight
was as iridescent as a rainbow.
She moved gracefully,
lifting a curious head
heavenward in space.
And, if she could not quite understand
what it was she feared,
she held some instinct true
within her considerable shape,
and perished in the sudden shelter
of an indeterminate fate.

THE LESARDE

At noon in the damp brush,
panting and hungry,
a lizard waits, momentarily
out of danger but afraid;
sunk in whatever wonder it knows
of the greatness of the beast,
which, rising from the swamp,
hesitates, tail lashing
across the mountain meadow.

Past and present recede,
but something is left there,
wedded to eternity; beyond them both.
This thing which remains,
remembers itself in time,
in the deep heart of a continent.
What sent them to destruction
in the sudden shelter
of their mutual fate?

Moon Shot, 1969

Driving through the mountains
toward Sun Valley, Idaho,
with the shadows falling,
suddenly there is a moon—
the moon, full of men
moving into the space of it.
A long distance, far
beyond the Sawtooths,
beyond the earth's edge,
beyond imagination.
Nevertheless I am closer,
here in these mountains,
high up, gazing upward,
marveling, moon struck.
I drive on into the mystery.
Stunned. Trying to know
the meaning of the beginning
of the end of my old world.

Tornado

The dark cloud rolls in across
the great open space,
like a curtain falling on a stage,
and fortified by lightning,
thunders like a herd
of a thousand bison on the plains.
Small white points reach down
toward the patient earth,
and the wind races high in the trees,
fleeing angry and furious.

    The blossoms of Catalpas
    run amuck in the leaves,
    frantically swinging their hats,
    like angels with bent wings.

Then suddenly . . . it is still,
and the land turns golden.
The peace and quiet . . . stillness
is a pause we listen to.
But it is only a moment
before the train rushes in,
and smashes the bright glory
of spring's early promise.

Vigilantes

Upon reading Walter Van Tilburg
Clark's *The Ox-Bow Incident.*

The men had gathered
their guns, their horses saddled,
heads together, restless against
the time . . .
It was coming up a storm.
Cloud shadows were moving fast.
A wind, swift above the ground,
made dark patches on the hills.
Gleams of sunlight came and left,
making the bridle buckles wink,
and lighting the big sign,
swinging and sagging
over the white veranda of the inn.

The wind pushed, fickle as a lover,
rushing men, flapping their garments,
blowing out the horses' tails
like plumes of dark smoke.
It was a heavy wind, damp and flawing down,
whistling its cold message
through the town, past the church,
as one by one, twenty-nine men
silently mounted their destiny
and headed into its fury.

Melville, Listen . . .

It is a clear, steel-blue day.
The pensive air is transparent,
pure and soft as a woman's look.
The robust and man-like sea
heaves in lingering swells,
and gliding on snow-white wings,
unspeckled birds sweep,
drifting on the breeze
far down the endless blue.

Aloft like a mighty czar,
the sun mounts the highest realms,
above this bold and rolling sea,
even as a groom his bride,
in soft and tremulous motion,
rides her bosom down,
uniting in a marriage
of song and love and power.

Sweet wonders of sky and air
that we should in laughter
heed the gambol of Nature,
sporting in youthful garb,
driving the daily shuttle,
as the weaver drives a loom,
so the weary life traveler
goes from weal to woe
under the winsome sky
to chance the rising tide.

Naias

The sea rises from a far stronghold,
and in giant heaves flings itself
crashing on the sandy beach.
Back and forth in fury,
it draws a long sweep
leaving foam-flecked lines
that rise and fall and sink.

Against the sky almost blue,
I see a girl riding naked
on a galloping horse,
both their manes flying
in the early mist.
Each hoof strikes a silvery path.
I love the girl, so free,
her dark hair flowing in the breeze
is touched by points of light.
A bit of tulle
has slipped over a slender breast,
and flings back a challenge.

I think of Helen,
so stately and beautiful,
so lovely in the rose-tipped dawn
my breath catches, and I know
why all the chieftains in Greece
had been her suitors:
why Paris abducted her,
and why the Trojan city fell.

Yet, here she rides again,
morning sun-sprung from her
father's amorous wanderings.

An Inner Light

These sea nymphs who ballet
on the crests of the sea
are the laughing ones,
the happy ones. Aphrodite,
born of that same sea foam,
won the golden apple,
bribed Paris,
and destroyed a golden city.

I would I had a girdle
such as Aphrodite wore.
Irresistible, enticing,
I too would hold sacred
the swan and dove and ram.

But no god of love
or beauty has more inner light
than the one I love.
I swear it by the erection
of the rose-tinted dawn,
shining on the mountains
where rivers from the snows
rush through the hills.
Such beauty enters the rooms
of my bursting desire.

A Texas Waltz

Waltzing across Texas, they say,
is a song and a dance.
I say it is a marvel
of changing vistas.
To go any place in Texas:
    Paris, Rome, London, Wells,
    Braunfels, El Paso del Norte,
    takes a while.

Longer than a song or dance.

Some places never heard of:
    Nacogdoches, Salado,
    Matamoros, Waxahachie,
    and Six-Shooter Junction.

People who rode ponies there:
    Karankawas and Tonkawas,
    Chief Karnate and the Caddoes,
    heroes of long ago.

And these:
    Captain Matthew [Old Paint] Caldwell,
    Houston, Crockett, et al
    on the long trails.

So many battles for Six Flags
    Plum Creek, Alamo, Goliad,
    The Great High Plains,
    and *The War.*

All of which now lie beneath
    Houston, Laredo, San Antonio,
    bluebonnets, wine cups,
    and the Indian paint brush.

Such a long waltz across.

Musings on Life and Death

From the seventh floor of Presbyterian Hospital,
you can see the sun rise over Dallas, Texas.
All the glass towers turn golden,
like the autumn leaves of New England.
An American flag flies above a Turkish dome
of a Christian church, an anomaly here
where they say, those who know, I guess,
that Baptists reign supreme.
Here in this sanctuary, medicine is certain.
Life comes and goes.

The Dallas sky during these fleeting moments
rests between first light and sunrise
when the air is wiped clean of all color,
between the first line of dawn
and the rising sun. I think of a bright day
in the rolling sandhills of Nebraska
where the Cheyenne and Sioux once chased the
Bison, and when Dull Knife's people
broke out of Fort Robinson on a cold,
snow-winter night and fled to freedom:
some to their deaths under a sky sprayed
with stars and the earth with blood.

Well below here, a border of pansies bends,
as if at Matins, beneath the delicate branches
of an ornamental willow that lifts bare limbs
as a breze sweeps the rooftops where
seven resting pigeons bend eyes sidewise,
watching ghosts walking in the early lights'
diffusion, before uncoiling swift wings,
as if pursued by the encroaching day,
when some weep happiness; others mourn.

Encycle

In the autumn of my days,
into my beyond time,
I take a space of the past,
before the future comes,
in reckoning a moment, seasons,
years and centuries.
Successive existence edges on eternity.
Is this then the strange land
traveled, passed through,
where magnificent distant domes
of onyx, chalcedony, pearl,
lapis lazuli and alabaster halls,
stand beside the river's silver,
and golden moments become again
the birth of the old cycle?
Is this the round of years,
of tears, events, phonemena?

My god the small intervals
of exaltation, passion, rapture,
midway between the extremes,
and all the lost dreams!

About the Author

Dorys Crow Grover is a native of Oregon and Professor Emerita, Department of Literature and Languages, Texas A&M University—Commerce, Texas. She is a published author and has been honored with several awards for poetry and short stories. In July 1989 she received the Fort Concho Centennial Award in Poetry for "The Ranch on the Limpia," published in *Concho River Review*. For the story "Paso Por Hombre," she was awarded the Llano Estacado *Southwest Heritage* Bill Leftwich Spanish Conquistador Hat statue in 1977. In 1990 she was named Distinguished Professor at a faculty awards meeting of the University. She resides in Campbell, Texas.